THEY FOUGHT FOR US:

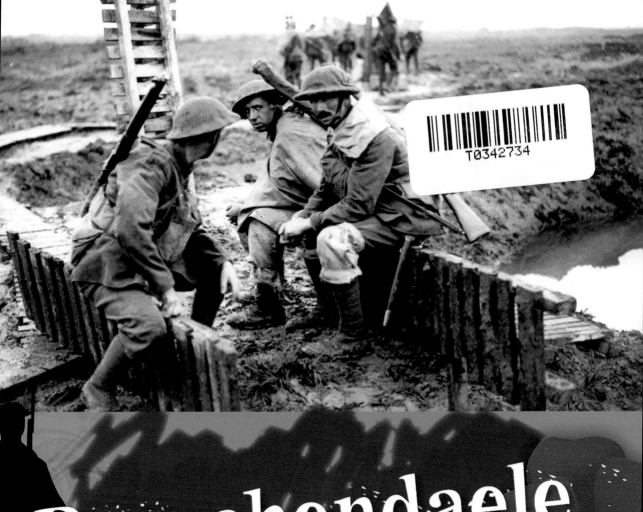

Passchendaele

Ruth Naumann

NELSON
CENGAGE Learning

Australia • Brazil • Japan • Korea • Mexico • Singapore • Spain • United Kingdom • United States

NELSON
CENGAGE Learning·

They Fought for Us: Passchendaele
1st Edition
Ruth Naumann

Cover design: Cheryl Rowe, Macarn Design
Text design: Cheryl Rowe, Macarn Design
Illustrations: Jamie Laurie
Production controller: Siew Han Ong
Reprint: Jess Lovell

Any URLs contained in this publication were checked for currency during the production process. Note, however, that the publisher cannot vouch for the ongoing currency of URLs.

Acknowledgements
Front cover: Photo courtesy of Pen and Sword Books Ltd. Back cover: Frank Hurley photograph courtesy of the National Library of Australia. Page 6: istock photograph courtesy of Mike Dabell. Page 14: photo courtesy of Pen and Sword Books Ltd. Pages 20, 24, 27, 29 and 45: Frank Hurley photographs courtesy of the National Library of Australia. Pages 27 and 40: photographs courtesy of the Kippenberger Military Archive, National Army Museum, Waiouru, New Zealand. Pages 46-48: photographs courtesy of the New Zealand Ministry of Defence. Page 44: image courtesy of The New Zealand Herald. The following photos are courtesy of Alexander Turnbull Library, Wellington, New Zealand: Page 8 (left): New Zealand soldiers passing the ruins of the Cloth Hall in Ypres, Belgium, 4 October 1917, 1/2 -013129-G; Page 8 (right): The ruins of Ypres Cathedral, Belgium, Henry Armytage Sanders, b 1886, 4 October 1917, G- 12949-1/2; Page 11: A battlefield in Menen in Belgium, 1917, 1/2-C-003260-F; Page 12: Gun crew at Burr Cross Roads, Western Front, between 1914 and 1918, PAColl-2667-006; Page 15: The New Zealand Rifle Brigade in camp near the line, World War I, 19 Sep 1917, 1/4-009490-G; Page 16 (top): The New Zealand signals office near the Western Front, World War I, 1917, 1/2-012884-G; Page 16 (middle): Members of the Pioneer Battalion laying a road in Messines, Belgium , 1917, 1/2-012772-G; Page 16 (bottom): New Zealand cooks prepare a meal for troops in the trenches, World War I , 29 Oct 1918, 1/2-013690-G; Page 17: General Alexander John Godley, 25 Aug 1917, 1/4-009477-G; Page 18 (top left): Farewell luncheon for World War 1 soldiers at Trentham camp, ca 1916, 1/2-106752-F; Page 18 (top right): Red Cross parcels, ca 1915, 1/1 -009356-G; Page 18 (bottom): Lipscombe, E J : Photograph of No.3 General Hospital, Codford in 1917, PAColl-7611; Page 26: New Zealand troops immediately returned from the line enjoy the luxury of a bath, 30 Jun 1917, 1/2-012815-G; Page 28 (top left): Rations on their way to the trenches, Dickebusch, World War I, 5 Feb 1918, 1/2-013053-G; Page 28 (top right): Issuing the rum ration to troops in the front trenches, World War I, 2 Feb 1918, 1/2-013056-G; Page 28 (middle): New Zealand soldiers make tea near the Wieltje Road, Ypres Salient, 18 Oct 1917, 1/2 -012937-G; Page 28 (bottom): Two men preparing sausage rolls for the Otago Battalion, Selles, France, 1917, 1/2-012965-G; Page 29 (bottom): New Zealand troops in the trenches, World War I, May 1917, 1/4 -009460-G; Page 30: Gater Point, on the battlefield near Zonnebeke, Ypres Sector, Belgium, during World War I, 24 October 1917, 1/2-C -003343-F; Page 32: New Zealand reinforcements near Kansas Farm, World War I, 13 October 1917, 1/2-012933-G; Page 33: Hellfire Corner, Passchendaele, Belgium, between 1914 and 1918, 1/2-051945-F; Page 35: Shells exploding in a trench during World War 1, between 1914 -1018, PAColl-4580-08; Page 36: German prisoners bringing in the wounded, Spice Farm, 4 October 1917, 1/2-012932-G; Page 37: New Zealand soldiers make tea near Wieltje Road, Ypres Salient, 18 October 1917,1/2-012937-G; Page 38: New Zealand troops on the way to the firing line in the St Jean sector, World War I, 11 Oct 1917, 1/2-012939-G; Page 39: World War I New Zealand Engineers resting in a large shell hole at Spree Farm, 12 Oct 1917, 1/2-012935; Page 40 (smaller): Mules carrying ammunition to the New Zealand guns on the Western Front, World War I, 12 Oct 1917, 1/2-012944-G; Page 41: Gun crew in mud at Passchendaele, ca 1917, PAColl-2667-014; Page 45: New Zealand troops crossing the Ypres Canal towards the front line, 18 Oct 1917, 1/2 -012929-G.

For product information and technology assistance,
in Australia call **1300 790 853**;
in New Zealand call **0800 449 725**

For permission to use material from this text or product, please email
aust.permissions@cengage.com

National Library of New Zealand Cataloguing-in-Publication Data
National Library of New Zealand Cataloguing-in-Publication Data

Naumann, Ruth.
Passchendaele (They fought for us)
ISBN 978-017018-053-5
1. Ypres, 3rd Battle of, Ieper, Belgium, 1917—Juvenile literature.
2. World War, 1914-1918—Campaigns—Belgium—Juvenile literature.
3. World War, 1914-1918—New Zealand—Juvenile literature.
4. Soldiers—New Zealand—Juvenile literature. [1. Ypres, 3rd Battle of, Ieper, Belgium, 1917. 2. World War, 1914-1918. 3. Soldiers.]
I. Title. II. Series: Naumann, Ruth. They fought for us.
940.431—dc 22

Cengage Learning Australia
Level 7, 80 Dorcas Street
South Melbourne, Victoria Australia 3205

Cengage Learning New Zealand
Unit 4B Rosedale Office Park
331 Rosedale Road, Albany, North Shore 0632, NZ

For learning solutions, visit **cengage.co.nz**

Printed in Australia by Ligare Pty Limited.
2 3 4 5 6 7 8 19 18 17 16 15

In the British Army, soldiers on foot were called infantry. Soldiers on horseback were called cavalry. The infantry was divided into groups with special names. For example, several battalions made a brigade, several brigades made a division, several divisions made a corps. Then there were groups within groups. For example, a division might have three infantry brigades and four artillery (big guns and gunners) brigades. Each group had its own leaders. A division leader was called a Major, a corps leader was called a Lieutenant-General. Numbers of men in groups varied but generally a division had about 18,000 men and officers.

BLOG: At the end of each unit in this book you will be asked to update your blog. A blog is a we**b log**. Many newspaper journalists now publish blogs but anyone can publish a blog. If you want to set up a real one and need advice on how, search the net under 'how to blog'. However, you may prefer to just keep a pretend blog in your own folder or notebook rather than a real one on the net.
A blog is an online journal where you put diary entries about your personal thoughts, opinions, experiences, ideas, suggestions, comments. An entry on your blog is called a post. You can post anything you like on your blog such as photos, web links, multimedia, graphics, documents. Like a newspaper article or an email, a post has a subject or title. It often has a time and date. A key feature of blogs is that they are updated regularly. The latest post is shown first. If your blog is not going on the net you will not need to worry about the order of your posts. Although it is meant for public consumption, you don't have to use your name - it can be anonymous. Readers can reply to your blog.

Contents

Western Front

Focus

- Events have causes and effects.
- People move between places which has results for people and places.
- People respond to challenges as individuals and groups.

- On August 3 1914 troops from Germany invaded Belgium. Germany wanted to invade France and thought it was easier to get through Belgium than through its own border with France.
- Belgium had refused to give Germany permission to go through it to get to France. The countries of Britain and France got armies ready to help Belgium. On August 4 they declared war on Germany.
- This began what was called The Great War, although today it is usually called World War I.
- Germany, Britain, France and Belgium are in Europe.

IRELAND

BRITAIN
(UNITED KINGDOM)

GERMANY

BELGIUM

FRANCE

E U R O P E 1 9 1 4

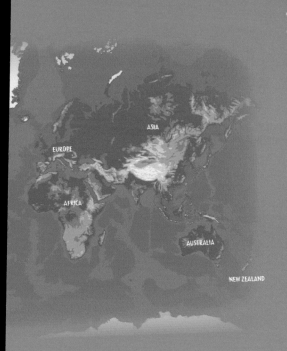

- New Zealand was a long way from Europe.
- New Zealand, however, had close links with Britain. It was part of the British Empire.
- The New Zealand government joined the war on the side of Britain and New Zealanders signed up to fight Germany. They fought under the command of Britain. Along with other Empire countries including Canada, Australia, India, and South Africa, New Zealanders were part of Allied forces or the 'Allies' – Britain, France and their friends.
- 102,438 New Zealanders left New Zealand to fight in World War I. Most served in Europe.
- 12,500 New Zealanders died in Europe. This was almost 10,000 more than the number of New Zealanders who died at Gallipoli.
- New Zealanders quickly learned where Belgium was on the world map. They felt sorry that Germany had invaded it and made many Belgian people homeless. They sent money, clothing, bedding and food such as sheep and apples to the people of Belgium.

Armies of Britain and France managed to stop Germans capturing Paris, the capital of France. The Germans wanted to hold on to parts they had captured of Belgium and France. They dug trenches for protection from advancing British and French troops.
The British and French knew they could not break through the German trenches so they began to dig trenches too.
Soon these trenches ran from the North Sea to Switzerland.
This system of trenches came to be called 'The Western Front'. The name came from the Germans. They had an Eastern Front in Russia.

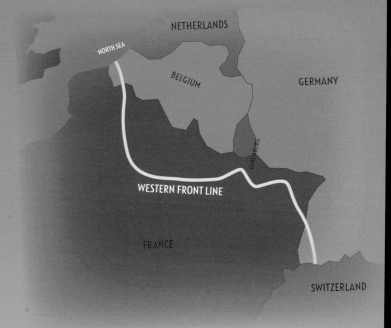

EXPLAIN/ DESCRIBE/ DISCUSS ... how the invasion of Belgium was an event with causes and results.

NET: Find an interactive map of Europe to help you learn the names and locations of countries in western Europe.

BLOG: Start your web log. Some features to consider could be - What would be a good title? Have you ever heard of Passchendaele and the Western Front? Why did New Zealand get involved in a European War?

Flanders

Focus

- People move between places which has results for people and places.
- Events have causes and effects.

- Flanders is the name of a region in the north of Belgium.
- The Western Front ran through Flanders. Many New Zealanders fought in Flanders.
- The land of Flanders was flat and soggy.
- Wet weather was common and thunderstorms could come at any time.
- October was usually the wettest month of the year. It meant the start of winter.

John McCrae of Canada wrote *In Flanders Fields* while he was a doctor in Flanders. John took a horse called Bonfire to the war. He sent his young nieces and nephews letters 'written' by Bonfire and signed with a hoof print. He saw how shells tore up the land of Flanders and how seeds of wild poppies sprouted in it. One day a shell killed his friend. This event resulted in one of the most famous pieces of writing in English. In the trenches during a pause in bombing next day, John McCrae wrote his poem.

In Flanders Fields

In Flanders fields the poppies blow
Between the crosses, row on row,
That mark our place; and in the sky
The larks, still bravely singing, fly
Scarce heard amid the guns below.

We are the Dead. Short days ago
We lived, felt dawn, saw sunset glow,
Loved, and were loved, and now we lie
In Flanders fields.

Take up our quarrel with the foe:
To you from failing hands we throw
The torch; be yours to hold it high.
If ye break faith with us who die
We shall not sleep, though poppies grow
In Flanders fields.

The poppy fields at Flanders.

NORTH SEA

NETHERLANDS

BRUGES

ANTWERP

GHENT

F L A N D E R S

GERMANY

YPRES

BRUSSELS

BELGIUM

FRANCE

LUXEMBURG

JOHN McCRAE
In early 1918 John was working at a military hospital in France when he died of pneumonia.
He was buried with full honours. Bonfire led John's funeral procession. John's riding boots
were carried back to front in the stirrups. This was a tradition to show that a warrior would
ride no more, and was looking back at his men for the last time.

EXPLAIN/ DESCRIBE/ DISCUSS ... how the movement of people around Flanders
had results for people and places.

NET: Find a picture of John McCrae.

BLOG: Update your blog.

Ypres

Focus

- People move between places which has results for people and places.
- Events have causes and effects.

- The Ypres area was described as being like a saucer. The town was in the middle where the cup sits. The surrounding land was the saucer rim. Before the war, the area was peaceful and had pretty farms.
- When German artillery shelled the town most of the townspeople fled.
- Ypres was an important place for New Zealand soldiers fighting in Flanders.
- Ypres is pronounced 'Eep'. Allied soldiers called it 'Wipers'. Today it is called 'Ieper'.
- It was a medieval town. Its famous Cloth Hall, begun in 1200, took one hundred years to build. World War I shells destroyed it quickly.
- Ypres was a key location. It was close to channel sea ports.
- Germans occupied Ypres for one night at the beginning of the war. Then the Allies captured it and held it. For the rest of the war thousands of soldiers from Britain and the British Empire, such as New Zealand, defended it.
- Millions of Allied soldiers passed through Ypres on the way to the front line.
- Even though shells destroyed Ypres, it stayed an important military centre for the Allies.
- However, Germans always wanted Ypres. The Kaiser (German king) told his German soldiers to capture Ypres or die.
- Saving Ypres from Germans was important to the Belgian people as it represented the last part of Belgium they had. It stood for Belgian pride.
- Ypres also became a symbol of the British Empire's determination to win the war.

New Zealand soldiers passing the ruins of the Cloth Hall in Ypres.

H306.

The ruins of Ypres Cathedral.

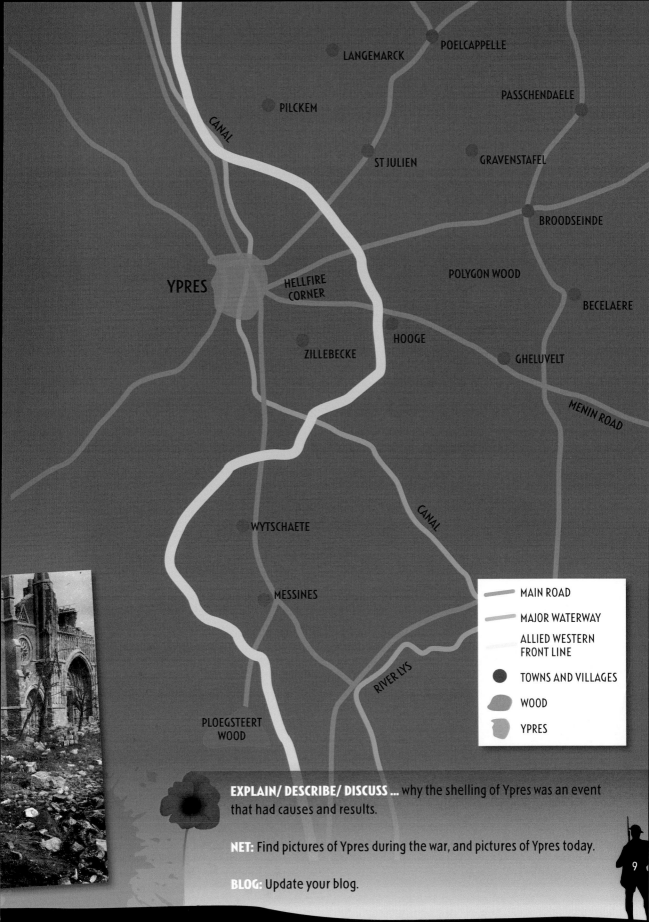

POELCAPPELLE

LANGEMARCK

PASSCHENDAELE

PILCKEM

CANAL

ST JULIEN

GRAVENSTAFEL

BROODSEINDE

YPRES

HELLFIRE CORNER

POLYGON WOOD

BECELAERE

HOOGE

ZILLEBECKE

GHELUVELT

MENIN ROAD

WYTSCHAETE

CANAL

MESSINES

RIVER LYS

PLOEGSTEERT WOOD

MAIN ROAD

MAJOR WATERWAY

ALLIED WESTERN FRONT LINE

TOWNS AND VILLAGES

WOOD

YPRES

EXPLAIN/ DESCRIBE/ DISCUSS ... why the shelling of Ypres was an event that had causes and results.

NET: Find pictures of Ypres during the war, and pictures of Ypres today.

BLOG: Update your blog.

9

Ypres Salient

Focus

- People move between places which has results for people and places.

- A salient is a big piece of land that juts out into territory held by the enemy. On a map it looks like a bulge in a line.
- The Ypres Salient was the area around Ypres held by the Allies.
- It meant Germans could fire at the Allies on three sides.
- The Ypres Salient was one of the most shelled places on Earth.
- Unlike other sectors on the Western Front, the Salient got action every day.
- Even in quiet times, thousands of men died and were wounded each month.
- The land in the salient was low-lying farmland. Belgian farmers had reclaimed this land from marsh by putting in drainage.
- The water table was near the surface, even during mid-summer.
- Shelling wrecked the drainage and caused the land to flood. More shelling turned the land into mud. Places where shells landed became craters and filled with mud and water.
- Shelling and rain turned little streams, such as the Steenbeek, into huge barriers.
- Allied trenches were on lower areas. German trenches and fortifications were on ridges.
- This meant Germans could see what was going on in the Salient and fire at Allied soldiers whenever and wherever they wanted.
- The Allies wanted to capture ridges and break out of the Salient.
- Germans wanted to capture the Salient and Ypres.
- Allied soldiers hated serving in the Salient. They could smell it long before they got to it. It stank of death and rotting bodies of men and horses.
- Often bodies were not buried for months. Shells often dug bodies up again.

The position of front lines changed after battles. For example, the Germans captured the village of St Julien in 1915 after they used chlorine gas against the Allied defenders.

STEENBEEK STREAM

PASSCHENDAELE

ALLIED FRONT LINE

BOESINGHE

ST JULIEN

THE YPRES SALIENT

HOOGE

GHELUVELT

MENIN ROAD

CANAL

WYTSCHAETE

MESSINES

The Ypres Salient was a dangerous place.

EXPLAIN/ DESCRIBE/ DISCUSS ... what the Ypres Salient was and why people moved in and out of it.

NET: Read five items about the Ypres Salient to help you make a map and description of the place.

BLOG: Update your blog.

Passschendaele

Focus
- People move between places which has results for the people and the places.

- Around the Salient were some raised areas of land. To New Zealanders, used to mountains and hills, these raised areas were just slopes. But to Europeans they were ridges.
- Passchendaele Ridge was the highest ridge in the area. On it was Passchendaele, a small town or village, 8km east of Ypres. Germans had captured Passchendaele. Passchendaele is known as Passendale today.

OSTEND

MIDDELKERKE

WESTENDE

NIEUPORT

FRONT LINE

WOOD

STEENSTRAAT

PASSCHENDAELE RIDGE

PASSCHENDAELE

GHELUVELT

MESSINES RIDGE

WYTSCHAETE

MESSINES

MENIN

Soldiers on duck

 HIGH GROUND

 WOOD

- Passchendaele Ridge was the last high ground before you hit open country. It was therefore precious to both Germans and Allies.
- Germans held Passchendaele Ridge, as well as other high ground in the area.
- Passchendaele was the best place in the area for Germans to see what was going on in the Ypres Salient.
- Because of this Germans had built a large number of fortifications all over the ridge.
- The British wanted the now ruined town of Passchendaele and ridge. To get them, their soldiers would have to advance uphill. German soldiers, hiding in their fortifications, would be able to shoot them easily.
- Because Germans were on higher land and had fortifications, they stayed a lot drier than Allied soldiers did.

Passchendaele was one of many places completely destroyed during the battles round Ypres. Nothing in Passchendaele was left. Farms, houses, woods, streams, trees were all ruined. For miles and miles, the area was a wasteland. People who live in Passendale today say they feel sad when they see photos of what happened to their town in World War I when it was caught in the middle of fighting soldiers from other countries.

Passchendaele is today a symbol for loss during war. Often, people refer to it as the 'Hell of Passchendaele'. There were four main reasons for this. Firstly, a huge number of soldiers lost their lives there. During the three and a half months of Passchendaele about one and a half million men, counting Germans as well, were involved. Both sides had soldiers in reserve ready to move in. A division might go to the front line and have so many soldiers killed, that it had to be pulled out and another division sent in. Some divisions went in only once, while others went in several times. Secondly, fighting was intense. Thirdly, environmental conditions were awful. Lastly, although it was only a small sector of the front line, an enormous number of Allied and German divisions fought there, including all four Canadian divisions, all five Australian divisions, and New Zealand's one and only division. Behind the infantry were supporting troops such as artillery, signals, and engineers. A division's infantry might be sent in for only a certain number of times whereas its artillery might be sent in more times.

EXPLAIN/ DESCRIBE/ DISCUSS ... why there was so much movement of people around Passchendaele.

NET: The word Passchendaele has become associated with a battlefield of mud and shell craters. Find ten pictures which show this association.

BLOG: Update your blog.

How Battles Got Named

Focus
- People move between places which has results for people and places.

After World War I ended in 1918, a British naming group was formed to decide on official names for all battles and actions during the war.

Officially there were four Battles of Ypres during World War I

First Battle of Ypres (October 19-November 22, 1914)
Germans tried to capture Ypres from the Allies. They failed.

Second Battle of Ypres (April 22-May 15, 1915)
Germans again tried to capture Ypres. They failed again.

Third Battle of Ypres (July 31-November 10, 1917)
Allies tried to capture Passchendaele Ridge. They finally did.

Fourth Battle of Ypres (April 9-April 29, 1918)
Germans tried to capture the Ypres Salient. They failed.

Battles within Battles
The four Battles of Ypres were all broken down into specific battles at various places. For example, the Third Battle of Ypres consisted of eight specific battles.

Gun crew at Passchendaele.

The Third Battle of Ypres
The Third Battle of Ypres, known as Third (3rd) Ypres, is also called Passchendaele. This is because the British aimed to break through German defences and capture Passchendaele Ridge and its ruined town. Third Ypres had eight battles.
- Pilckem Ridge (July 31-August 2)
- Langemarck (August 16-18)
- Menin Road (September 20-25)
- Polygon Wood (September 26-October 3)
- **Broodseinde (October 4)**
- Poelcappelle (October 9)
- **First Passchendaele (October 12)**
- Second Passchendaele (October 26-November 10)

The New Zealand Division took part in two of these battles – Broodseinde and First Passchendaele. First Passchendaele is usually simply called Passchendaele. As Passchendaele is also used for Third Ypres, this causes confusion.

EXPLAIN/ DESCRIBE/ DISCUSS ... how the four battles of Ypres were events that each had a main caus and a main result.

NET: The Battle of Messines was a famous battle that took place just before Passchendaele. The New Zealand Division was part of its stunning success. Find out what happened. For example, a key featur was the detonation of 19 big mines in tunnels secretly dug under Germans.

BLOG: Update your blog.

New Zealand Division

Focus

- People respond to challenges as individuals and groups.
- People move between places which has results for people and places.
- Cultural interaction impacts on cultures and societies.

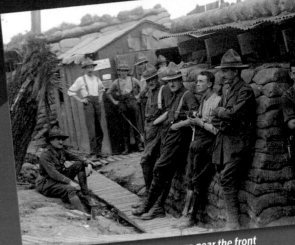

The New Zealand Rifle Brigade in camp near the front line on September 19 1917.

Many New Zealand males responded to the challenge of war by becoming soldiers.

In 1914 almost eight and a half thousand volunteers left New Zealand to fight for Britain. In Egypt they, and the Australian soldiers, were organised into divisions. There were not enough New Zealanders to make a separate division so they joined Australians who were not in the Australian Division. Later, so many reinforcements from New Zealand arrived that a New Zealand Division was formed.

From Sling training camp in England, soldiers were able to go as tourists to places like London, which had a New Zealand Soldiers' Club and a New Zealand YMCA facility. At camps soldiers trained by throwing bombs, coping with gas attacks, building wire entanglements, getting bayonets on and off rifles, and operating Lewis machine-guns. Some got in trouble for giving cheek to instructors or not paying enough attention to authority and uniform. Their pay rate began at four shillings a day; the British rate began at one shilling. On arrival at camp their paybooks, along with haircuts and hobnail boots, were checked. Soldiers got Kiwi brand tins of nugget with which to polish boots. This was another feature which helped identify them as Kiwis.

In May 1916, the New Zealand Division sailed to France. They went close to Armentières, which was near the Belgian border and about three kilometres behind the Allied front line. There the division began its Western Front experience of trench warfare. Armentières was a big town. During a 1918 German attack it was flattened. In 1916 however, much of its population was still there. Soldiers were surprised to see people still working in fields.

On the Western Front soldiers were in camps or billets in towns and villages until they had a spell in trenches. In Flanders they were able to visit cafes known as estaminets where they chatted up local girls. They called British soldiers 'Tommies' and German soldiers 'Fritz', 'Hun', or 'Boche' or 'Bosche'. In the trenches they needed steel helmets. Away from the fighting, they pushed their soft hats into the shape of a lemon-squeezer which distinguished them from other soldiers.

EXPLAIN/ DESCRIBE/ DISCUSS ... some cultural effects of the movement of the New Zealand Division to the Western Front.

NET: Find out how New Zealand got soldiers throughout the period of war, 1914-18.

BLOG: Update your blog.

A Group of Specialists

Focus
- People respond to challenges as individuals and groups.

H184

The New Zealand Division was not just foot soldiers, known as infantry. There were other specialist groups such as Mounted Rifles, Engineers, a Cycle Company, Medical Corps, Army Service, Butchery, Bakery, Veterinary.

By the time of Passchendaele enough Maori reinforcements had arrived at the Western Front to make a complete (Maori) Pioneer Battalion. It was the labour force of the New Zealand Division. Its men built light railways, tramlines, trenches and roads.

H61

Soldiers in 1917 had no computers or mobile phones. Wireless was still primitive. They had to rely on semaphore, morse code, signal lamps, homing pigeons, runners, telephone, and telegraph.

Motor vehicles were no use in mud. Thousands and thousands of horses and mules went to the Western Front. Many horses were shipped from New Zealand. They hauled guns and supplies. Many were killed and wounded. A constant problem was finding enough grain, or even sawdust cake, for them. They were always hungry. Soldiers felt sad when they saw horses trying to eat wagon wheels. Horses came to know when a shell was approaching; they trembled and tried to bury their muzzles in the chests of soldiers. The scream of a shell could make a horse twitch. Horses suffered from shell shock.

H11

Top to bottom: The New Zealand signals office near the Western Front. One soldier is sending morse code and the other minds the telephone system; The Pioneer Battalion making a road; New Zealand cooks prepare a meal for troops in the trench

EXPLAIN/ DESCRIBE/ DISCUSS ... how individuals who responded to the challenge of war became groups.

NET: A famous battle that New Zealanders were involved in on the Western Front before Passchendaele was the Somme. Find out when and where it was, and what happened.

BLOG: Update your blog.

Leaders of New Zealanders

Focus

- Leadership of groups has results for communities and societies.

The leader of British armies at the Western Front was Field Marshal Sir Douglas Haig. He was said to be hard-working and determined, but with no imagination or humour. Soldiers called him 'Butcher Haig'. They thought he did not care how many of them died carrying out his plans. Haig did argue that any German loss of men was more important than British loss of men because Allies could take more losses since America had joined the war. He did not see the conditions at Passchendaele. When Passchendaele was finally over, Haig's chief-of-staff visited the area for the first time. It was reported that as his car tried to get through mud around Passchendaele, he burst into tears. 'Good God,' he said. 'Did we really send men to fight in that?' Haig dismissed him.

General Alexander John Godley.

Haig had two British armies fighting at Passchendaele. One was the British 2nd Army. It was led by General Sir Herbert Plummer. After two years in the Ypres Salient his hair went completely white. Part of the British 2nd Army was II Anzac Corps. It was led by General Sir Alexander Godley. Godley was an Englishman. New Zealand soldiers did not like him as he had been at Gallipoli. New Zealand's one and only division, The New Zealand Division, was part of the II Anzac Corps. It was led by Major General Andrew Russell. He was born in New Zealand.

Haig was and is called a controversial figure because of controversy (argument) over his leadership. One side of the argument says he should never have sent soldiers to capture places like Passchendaele when there was little chance of success. The other side defends his actions.

Major General Andrew Russell visited the front line often. After things went horribly wrong at Passchendaele on October 12 1917 he accepted blame. Some experts said the main blame lay further up the chain of command.

The General, by Siegfried Sassoon

"Good morning, good morning!" the General said
When we met him last week on our way to the line.
Now the soldiers he smiled at are most of them dead,
And we're cursing his staff for incompetent swine.
"He's a cheery old card," grunted Harry to Jack
as they slogged up to Arras with rifle and pack.
But he did for them both by his plan of attack.

[Arras = name of a town close to the front line]

EXPLAIN/ DESCRIBE/ DISCUSS ...how leadership can affect soldiers.

NET: Collect differing opinions about Field Marshal Sir Douglas Haig.

BLOG: Update your blog.

Girls and Women Help

Focus

- People respond to challenges as individuals and groups.
- Events have causes and effects.
- People move between places which has results for people and places.

Soldiers on the Western Front knew they had help and support from New Zealand girls and women. They may have received photos like the ones on this page.

Top to bottom, left to right: Members of the Spinsters Club knitting socks for World War I soldiers; Farewell lunch for soldiers at Trentham Camp in New Zealand; Women in Nelson packing hospital supplies for soldiers; New Zealand nurses worked in hospitals set up in France and England for New Zealand soldiers. When Germans shelled hospitals, nurses had to wear steel hats. Some New Zealand nurses worked close to the front line. Sister Kemp was killed in October 1917 when a plane bombed the casualty clearing station she was working at in Flanders.

EXPLAIN/ DESCRIBE/ DISCUSS ... how New Zealand girls and women responded to war.

NET: Find and read an account from a nurse who nursed New Zealand soldiers in the wa

BLOG: Update your blog.

Haig's Plan

Focus
- Leadership of groups has results for communities.
- Events have causes and effects.

ZEEBRUGGE

Germany captured the Belgian ports of Ostend and Zeebrugge. German U-boats (submarines) based there attacked Allied shipping. By 1917, Germany still had not broken through Allied trenches on the Western Front. It thought that if its U-boats could stop ships getting supplies to Britain, it could starve the British. This would force Britain to surrender. Haig decided U-boats had to be stopped, whatever the cost.

OSTEND

Haig was a cavalry man – he believed in soldiers on horses. He said modern weapons such as aeroplanes, tanks, and barbed wire were only aids to horses and men. The machine gun, he thought, was much over-rated. His plan was for foot-soldiers, infantry, to drive Germans off Passchendaele and surrounding ridges. Then he would send in cavalry to chase Germans all the way to the sea. Once Allies had driven Germans away from the Belgian coast and captured the ports of Ostend and Zeebrugge, Allies would then be able to threaten Germany itself, especially its industrial heartland in the Ruhr.

WESTERN FRONT LINE

PASSCHENDAELE

YPRES

Field Marshall Sir Douglas Haig

In May 1917, French soldiers on the Western Front line mutinied. Thousands left trenches and went to the rear. They refused to go back to the front. Haig thought a British attack would draw attention away from the weakened French line. He also thought that a British victory would boost French morale.

Haig believed the war could be won only on the Western Front and by mainly British armies. For a long time he had wanted to launch a big attack on Germans in Flanders. He decided 1917 was the time. He planned to attack Germans from Ypres. His soldiers would capture the ridge at Passchendaele. This was the key to the whole area. Haig was prepared to keep sending soldiers in as replacements for those killed. He believed Germans were almost beaten and a big push would knock them over.

EXPLAIN/ DESCRIBE/ DISCUSS ... how and why a military leader might regard and use soldiers as resources.

NET: Find pictures and descriptions of the weapons used on the Western Front.

BLOG: Update your blog.

Telling Their Story

Focus

- People pass on and look after culture and heritage.
- People move between places which has results for people and places.
- Ideas and actions of people in the past impact on lives and identities.

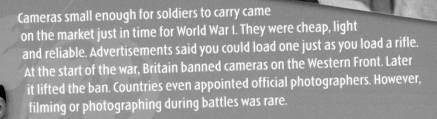

The movement of the New Zealand Division to the Western Front, and to the Passchendaele area, was an important event that impacted on many New Zealand families. It resulted in the story of Passchendaele being passed down through generations as part of the heritage of New Zealand. Soldiers told their story in photographs, letters and diaries, paintings and drawings, newspaper articles, and poetry. Later, other people wrote articles and books about Passchendaele.

Cameras small enough for soldiers to carry came on the market just in time for World War I. They were cheap, light and reliable. Advertisements said you could load one just as you load a rifle. At the start of the war, Britain banned cameras on the Western Front. Later it lifted the ban. Countries even appointed official photographers. However, filming or photographing during battles was rare.

Poets wrote poems about the war. Here is an extract from a British poet, Siegfried Sassoon. Duckboards were boards that soldiers put over mud so they could walk on them. They looked like boards put down for ducks to get from river banks up to duckhouses.

> I died in Hell - they called it Passchendaele;
> my wound was slight
> and I was hobbling back; and then a shell
> burst slick upon the duckboards; so I fell
> into the bottomless mud, and lost the light.

One thing the camera could not capture was the smell of war. It sickened soldiers new to the Western Front. They recorded it in letters and diaries. Bodies of men and horses lay rotting. Latrines overflowed. Soldiers sprayed cresol or chloride of lime around as disinfectant. Water in craters got putrid, mud reeked, sandbags decayed. Poison gas, cigarette and pipe smoke, cooking smells and cordite from exploded shells hung in the air. Soldiers went without baths for weeks or even months.

New Zealand appointed three official war artists. The British War Office let artists go close to battles but censored their pictures the same way they did letters from soldiers.

Malcom Ross became an official war correspondent in 1915. He was with the New Zealand Division on the Western Front until the end of the war. He spent as much time as possible close to the battlefield. At first he was not allowed to cable news because the government said it cost too much.

After the war, authors wrote books and articles about Passchendaele. An example is Glyn Harper's book called *Massacre at Passchendaele*.

New Zealand History online has a lot of material about Passchendaele. Other sites such as Auckland Museum and Alexander Turnbull Library have photographs that you can access.

EXPLAIN/ DESCRIBE/ DISCUSS ... why soldiers kept records such as diaries and photographs and why those records became part of New Zealand's heritage and culture.

NET: Find some resources from New Zealand soldiers at Passchendaele.

BLOG: Update your blog.

Impact on the Environment

Focus

• People move between places which has results for people and places.

One result of soldiers moving to fight on the Western Front was the impact on the environment. Belgian farmers would never have imagined that one day soldiers from New Zealand would dig and live in trenches in Belgian soil.

Because Germans were the first to dig trenches they chose higher ground. Allies had to dig trenches on lower ground. This meant Allied soldiers had to fight not only Germans, but also water and mud in their trenches. As in Gallipoli, so much digging by New Zealand and Australian soldiers earned them their nickname of 'Diggers'.

New Zealanders had used trenches in Gallipoli but trenches here were different. There was space to build a more complicated system of trenches. They were in zigzag patterns. This meant that if a shell landed in one, shrapnel did not travel so far. It was also harder for Germans to get accurate co-ordinates for artillery strikes.

Behind front line trenches were support trenches. They were all joined up together by other trenches. Soldiers also dug temporary trenches. When a major attack was planned, they dug assembly trenches near the front trench. These gave shelter for waves of attacking soldiers who were to follow the first waves leaving front line trenches.

Beyond front line trenches were barbed wire entanglements and wire obstacles. They had a few breaks in them to let soldiers, though hopefully not enemy ones, move through.

The most dangerous place to be was in a listening post. This was often a shell hole in front of the barbed wire. A few soldiers would lie there and listen for an enemy attack so they could alert their own side. If the attack came, listeners would be lucky to survive. The enemy could also sneak up and capture listeners to try to get information out of them.

In front of the barbed wire was no-man's-land, the area between the two enemies.

This stylised drawing of a trench system shows how the front line trench had support trenches behind it. Behind the support trenches, there may have been more support trenches. Behind them was the artillery with more trenches leading off to ammunition depots and supply lines. Drawings make trenches look hygienic, tidy, well-built and safe places. Trenches were none of these things. Above all, drawings can not show the awful smell of dead bodies and excrement.

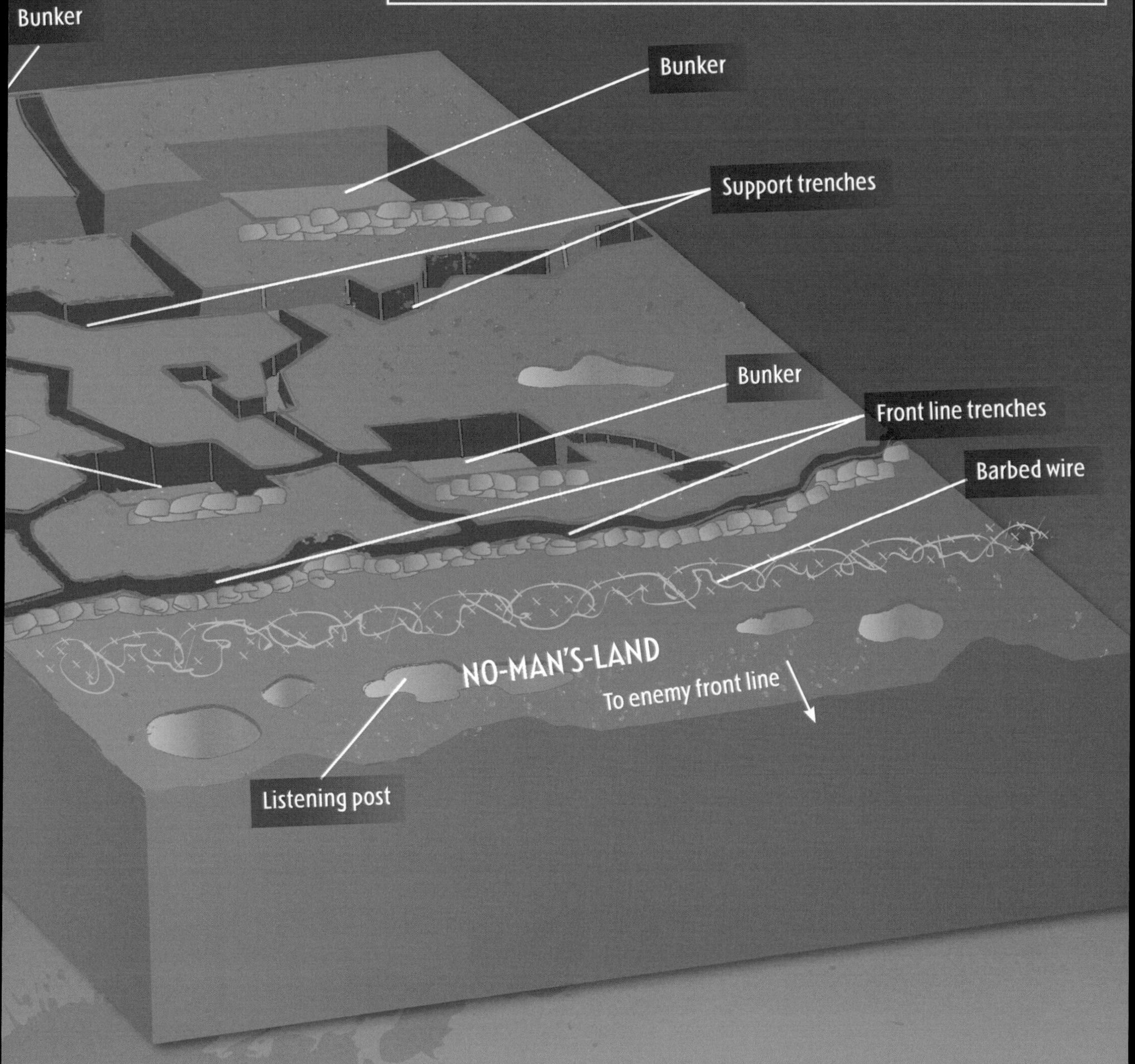

Bunker

Bunker

Support trenches

Bunker

Front line trenches

Barbed wire

NO-MAN'S-LAND

To enemy front line

Listening post

EXPLAIN/ DESCRIBE/ DISCUSS ... the impact of trenches on the environment.

NET: Small night patrols were sent into no-man's-land to get information about the enemy. Find out how German light-shell rockets helped Germans kill soldiers on night patrol. Also find photographs of no-man's-land.

BLOG: Update your blog.

Trenches

Focus
- People move between places which has results for people and places.

Dugout: Area dug out from wall of trench for one or more soldiers.

Sandbags: Protect parados and parapet.

Periscope: To let soldiers see over the top of the trench without getting their heads blown off. It could be just a stick with two angled mirrors at top and bottom.

Parados: Rear side of trench. Higher than front side.

Corpses: Problem if previous tenants buried them in bottom and sides of trench and new tenants dig into them.

Loophole: It might be ju a gap in sandbags, or it might be fitted with a s plate. Lets soldiers see fire out of trench.

Pump: Sucks out water.

Parapet: Front side of tre

Water and mud: Constant problems.

Firestep: Step on parapet for sentries to stand on and for soldiers to stand on to shoot at enemy. Used by all soldiers when standing-to (waiting for expected enemy attack).

Duckboards: Boards put down to try to keep feet dry.

Breastworks: Mounding up, to provide protection, of any material found in the area such as earth, sandbags, rocks, bits of trees. Usually breast-high, but can be much higher.

Dugout: Space left in breastworks for shelter. Roofed.

Trench: Shallow ditch behind to drain water.

Attacks on the enemy were most common at dawn and dusk. At both times soldiers were at Stand-to. This was when they guarded against attacks by standing on the fire step with their bayonets fixed. After dawn Stand-to, soldiers would have breakfast, get ready for inspections, do chores such as draining water from the trench, take personal time for writing letters and sleeping. After Stand-to at dusk, the cover of darkness allowed jobs such as collecting rations, water and ammunition. Patrols might creep into no-man's-land with blacked faces, badges removed from their uniforms, and edges of bayonets dulled to stop them shining. Favourite raiding weapons were revolvers, and clubs called knobkerries hanging from wrists on leather thongs. Night was also when fresh soldiers arrived to replace those in the trenches.

EXPLAIN/ DESCRIBE/ DISCUSS ...the possible impact on soldiers of the first night in a trench.

NET: Find pictures of trenches, breastworks and dugouts.

BLOG: Update your blog.

Results of Life in a Trench

Rotting bodies of soldiers, and food scraps attracted rats. They swarmed through trenches, spreading disease and spoiling food. Some were nearly as big as cats. Soldiers woke to find rats running over their faces, nibbling at their ears, taking food out of their pockets, or fighting over bits of human flesh. Rats burrowed into corpses by starting at the eyes; they would eat a wounded man if he could not defend himself. Soldiers threw empty tins over the sides of trenches. If there was a quiet moment at night they could hear rats turning tins over. Soldiers tried shooting, bayonetting and clubbing rats. Soldiers were outnumbered however, because one rat pair could produce up to 900 offspring a year.

Water in shell holes, trenches and craters brought frogs. Soldiers could slip on them. Other trench creatures included red slugs and horned beetles.

Lice left blotchy red bite marks all over the body, caused terrible itching and a sour, stale smell. Lice also carried trench fever. Soldiers spent hours scratching and killing lice. They squashed them with fingernails and burned them with lit candles. They called lice-hunting 'chatting'. People from home sent tins of powder supposed to kill lice but it did not work. Sometimes soldiers were treated to baths in vats of hot water while their clothes were put through delousing machines. Some eggs stayed in the clothes, however, and within a few hours body heat hatched them out.

Trench fever caused shooting pains and high fever. It did not kill soldiers but stopped them being able to fight. Recovery away from trenches took up to three months. Nobody realised until 1918 that lice caused the fever.

Soldiers standing for hours in waterlogged trenches, unable to take off wet socks and boots, could get Trench foot. Feet swelled and went so numb they could not feel a bayonet stuck into them. Skin went red or blue. If the swelling started to go down, pain made soldiers cry or scream. If gangrene set in, doctors would have to cut off feet.

Antibiotics had not been discovered. Common infections were typhus, dysentery, cholera. Many soldiers died from exposure to cold. There was no proper sanitation. Trench toilets, or latrines, were usually pits dug at the end of a short trench. Sometimes soldiers had no time to dig new latrines so they used a nearby shell hole, or trenches. If supplies of water to trenches did not arrive, soldiers had to refill water bottles from dirty water in shell holes. Such water could cause dysentery.

Soldiers in a supply trench.

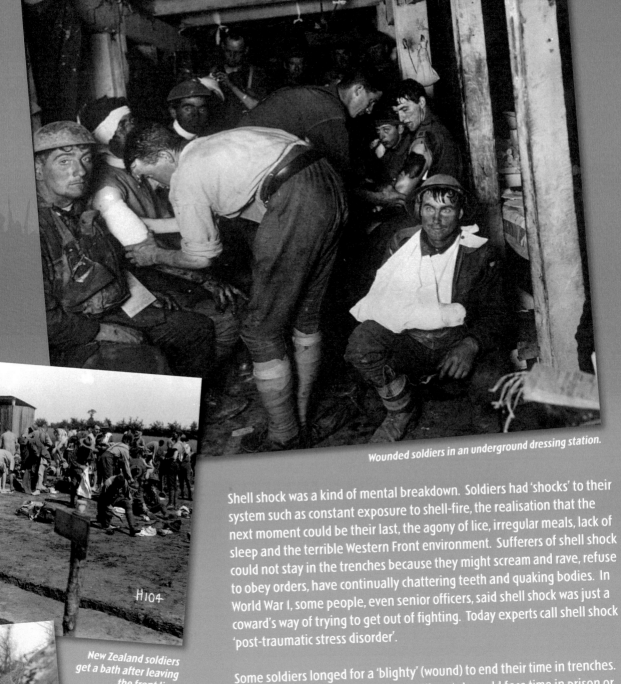

Wounded soldiers in an underground dressing station.

New Zealand soldiers get a bath after leaving the front line.

H104

Shell shock was a kind of mental breakdown. Soldiers had 'shocks' to their system such as constant exposure to shell-fire, the realisation that the next moment could be their last, the agony of lice, irregular meals, lack of sleep and the terrible Western Front environment. Sufferers of shell shock could not stay in the trenches because they might scream and rave, refuse to obey orders, have continually chattering teeth and quaking bodies. In World War I, some people, even senior officers, said shell shock was just a coward's way of trying to get out of fighting. Today experts call shell shock 'post-traumatic stress disorder'.

Some soldiers longed for a 'blighty' (wound) to end their time in trenches. Those who wounded themselves deliberately could face time in prison or execution by firing-squad. Some soldiers killed themselves, or stood on the fire-step so the enemy could shoot them.

EXPLAIN/ DESCRIBE/ DISCUSS … the impact of these issues on soldiers.

NET: Find descriptions of shell shock and how it was treated in World War I. Check out the story of three New Zealand privates who served on the Western Front and were executed, but honoured in 2005 for their war service. Find pictures of Trench Foot.

BLOG: Update your blog.

Feeding Soldiers

Focus

- People move between places which has results for people and places.

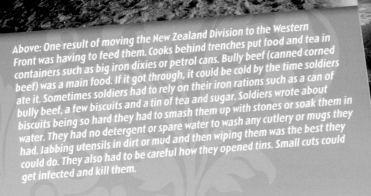

Above: One result of moving the New Zealand Division to the Western Front was having to feed them. Cooks behind trenches put food and tea in containers such as big iron dixies or petrol cans. Bully beef (canned corned beef) was a main food. If it got through, it could be cold by the time soldiers ate it. Sometimes soldiers had to rely on their iron rations such as a can of bully beef, a few biscuits and a tin of tea and sugar. Soldiers wrote about biscuits being so hard they had to smash them up with stones or soak them in water. They had no detergent or spare water to wash any cutlery or mugs they had. Jabbing utensils in dirt or mud and then wiping them was the best they could do. They also had to be careful how they opened tins. Small cuts could get infected and kill them.

Above right, top to bottom: Soldiers got a rum ration from earthenware jars, stamped with the initials S.R.D. This stood for Supply Reserve Depot. Soldiers claimed it stood for Service Rum Diluted, or Seldom Reaches Destination or Soon Runs Dry.
Soldiers liked tea. After marching, or working for hours at jobs such as carting ammunition and being ready to collapse into the mud rather than face the slog back to trenches, they might be greeted by a canteen waiting to give them a cup of tea and biscuits. Or they might take a break to make tea themselves.
Funds raised in New Zealand helped give soldiers treats such as meat pies or sausage rolls.

EXPLAIN/ DESCRIBE/ DISCUSS ... why the supply of food and hot drinks to soldiers was so important

NET: Find out what happens to food supplies during war-time.

BLOG: Update your blog.

Weapons

Focus

• People move between places which has results for people and places.

World War I aircraft.

When the war started, aircraft were still primitive. Built of wood and canvas, they could not fly far or fast. For the first two years of the war, enemy pilots, flying planes that were observors and not armed, waved at each other. Later, pilots tried hurling rocks, steel darts or grenades at the other plane or taking potshots with rifles. The German Fokker plane equipped with machine guns and associated with The Red Baron, did not appear on the Western Front until later on in the war. Bombers were slow and unreliable. Fighting at Passchendaele usually took place in bad weather which stopped planes going up. Some soldiers, however, mentioned seeing a German observor plane at Broodseinde on October 4.

New Zealand soldiers in a trench. Soldiers had grenades, rifles, bayonets, and rounds of ammunition. Only officers got pistols. Soldiers made sure their rifles were not clogged with mud. They also had spades or picks, for digging trenches. Many preferred to sharpen the blade of their spades and use them instead of bayonets. The spade's shorter handle made it easier to use in a trench against the enemy.

EXPLAIN/ DESCRIBE/ DISCUSS ... what the Western Front would have looked like at the end of the war.

NET: A German who served at Passchendaele was Erich Remarque, author of *All Quiet on the Western Front* which is a famous war novel. Another was the Red Baron who shot down several British planes there. Find out what happened to these two men and what Germans thought of Passchendaele.

BLOG: Update your blog.

Gas and Pillboxes

Focus

- People move between places which has results for people and places.

Captured German pillbox.

Soldiers always had to look out for gas. After the first German gas attacks, Allied soldiers were supplied with masks of cotton pads soaked in urine. Later they got proper gas masks. Chlorine gas destroyed respiratory organs and caused slow death by asphyxiation. The worst gas was Mustard gas. It had almost no smell and hung about in low areas for hours, even days. Once in the earth, it stayed active for weeks. It polluted drinking water. It clung to uniforms and boots. A soldier who jumped into a shell-hole for cover could end up blinded, with blistered skin and bleeding lungs. His body would be so painful that he might have to be strapped to a bed while he took several weeks to die. He might appear to recover, only to die much later from complications. At Flanders, gas blinded for a while a young German soldier called Adolf Hitler.

Pillboxes were baby forts. They could house from one to fifty men. New Zealanders called them pillboxes because they were the same shape as boxes in which chemists put tablets. They were low rectangles with narrow slits in walls to fire through. However, a slit was also a good place for a New Zealander to throw a grenade. Built of concrete reinforced with steel, they were hard to destroy. They protected Germans from artillery bombardments. A cunning feature was that the back walls were thinner and weaker. If New Zealanders captured a pillbox, Germans might be able to kill or kick out new owners by attacking from the rear. During an offensive Germans put machine-guns on top or at the sides of pillboxes and camouflaged them. Germans built thousands of pillboxes to make their trench lines stronger and to defend ridges around Passchendaele. Some were even built into ruined farmhouses and cattleyards left by fleeing Belgians. This helped disguise them. The British Army built very few machine-gun pillboxes. They said it was not worth the labour or cost. Some people suggested the real reason was the Army did not want soldiers getting comfortable inside pillboxes and therefore being unwilling to get out and attack Germans. Many pillboxes were individually marked on detailed battle maps and given names to identify them such as Anzac, Kit and Kat. A captured German pillbox might contain German schnapps and whisky.

EXPLAIN/ DESCRIBE/ DISCUSS ... the possible impact of gas and pillboxes on soldiers.

NET: Private Laurence Patrick Donohue from Papanui was one of many New Zealanders who died from complications due to mustard gas. As a member of the New Zealand Field Ambulance Company, his job was to help the wounded at Passchendaele. Find out what happened to him and his twin brother.

BLOG: Update your blog.

Stretcher-Bearers

Focus
- People move between places which has results for people and places.

Soldiers knew that after they went over the top or over the bags, which meant they climbed out of trenches to advance on German lines, they were not allowed to stop to look after wounded mates. For their own wounds, they had emergency field-dressings of bandages and pins. If they could move, they might crawl into a shell hole although they could drown there. They might lie in no-man's-land for days before stretcher-bearers found them.

Soldiers knew that in the coming battle they might owe their lives to stretcher-bearers, those heroes who walked under enemy fire. In the Passchendaele mud stretcher-bearers showed how strong the human spirit could be. Soldiers knew that even though these men would keep going out to collect wounded until they collapsed from exhaustion, there may not be enough stretchers to go round. Some dressing stations at Passchendaele gave little protection against German shells. If the dressing station was full, wounded would have to lie outside in mud. With rain, cold and maybe enemy fire upon them, many soldiers would die.

Soldiers also knew it might take several hours for stretcher-bearers to carry wounded behind front line trenches to aid posts, dressing stations or casualty clearing stations. During that time soldiers could die of the shock of shattered bone ends grinding together. Even if bearers got them to safety, they might have to cope with further shock as nurses or doctors tried to get them out of their khaki uniforms that would be solid slabs of mud.

EXPLAIN/ DESCRIBE/ DISCUSS ... the impact of these issues on soldiers.

NET: Find photos of stretcher-bearers at the Western Front.

BLOG: Update your blog.

New Zealand Division moves to Ypres Salient

Focus

- People move between places which has results for people and places.
- Events have causes and effects.

On September 24 1917 the New Zealand Division was ordered to move to the Ypres battle area. They marched for six days, moving 20 miles (32 km) per day. Although they kept to the regulation three miles per hour they still had to look out for German planes wanting to bomb them and their camps.

Soldiers needed strong backs. Even going over the bags they had to carry their gear. This might include a rifle with bayonet, wire cutters, field-dressing, spade, greatcoat, rolled ground sheet, water bottle, mess tin, towel, shaving kit, extra socks, gas mask, message book, and iron rations. For an attack they were given extra equipment such as sandbags, extra rations, bag of Mills grenades, and a couple of hundred rounds of ammunition. The weight of gear made it hard to move fast in good weather, let alone the mud they were to meet soon.

A stream of lorries with material for the front passed the New Zealand Division as they marched. Two and a half miles (4 km) away, the smell of the front hit them. They marched through the ruined town of Ypres and into the Salient. Conditions got worse and worse. Roads ceased to exist. Dead bodies from previous battles still lay on the ground amongst litter – shells, boots, packs, rifles, watches, helmets, glasses, false teeth, water bottles. Shell holes ran into other shell holes making craters filled with filthy water. Not a single tree stood; a few shattered stumps showed where a wooded area had been. Every farm was wrecked. Every field was torn up. Not one blade of grass remained. Piles of bricks showed where a farmhouse or village once stood. Tanks were stuck in black mud. Dead horses lay bloated and rotting.

New Zealand soldiers move in towards the front line in the Yypres Salient. At the moment they are on a road. Soon they will be on slippery boards built over mud dee enough to drown them if they fall off.

Hellfire Corner, like all roads around Ypres, was a heavily-shelled place.

On the evening of October 2, 4th and 1st New Zealand Brigades took over the trenches. 1st Canterbury and 1st Otago of 2nd Brigade remained in the forward area as reserves. The rest went back to divisional reserve. 2nd Brigade Machine Gun Company remained in the line.

On the evening of October 3, gale-force winds and rain arrived. Troops huddled in assembly trenches and tried to sleep.

EXPLAIN/ DESCRIBE/ DISCUSS ... how Haig's plan of attack caused the movement of New Zealand soldiers.

NET: Find out what gear New Zealand soldiers carried at the Western Front.

BLOG: Update your blog.

33

Plan for Battle of Broodseinde

Focus
- People move between places which has results for people and places
- Events have causes and effects.

The New Zealand Division had only a few days to prepare for action on October 4. They worked hard and by October 2 all guns of the New Zealand Artillery were forward in their new positions. The guns were ready to fire and had plenty of ammunition. In support of the New Zealanders were 180 18-pounders, 60 4.5 inch howitzers and 68 machine guns. At the Western Front artillery used a technique called 'creeping barrage'. This involved artillery extending their range at timed intervals so they did not hit their own soldiers who could advance under artillery protection.

The plan was 'bite and hold'. Taking German positions was 'bite'. Quickly digging trenches and defending positions against German attack was 'hold'.

The attack was made by twelve Divisions on a 13km front. Four Anzac Divisions in the middle were the spearhead of the attack. II Anzac Corps, containing New Zealand Division, was to take Gravenstafel Spur. Close by was a small crest given the name Abraham Heights by Canadians from a previous battle. Further on and separated from Gravenstafel Spur by a small stream called the Ravebeek, which later merged into the Strombeek, was Bellevue Spur. Germans had both spurs protected by hidden pillboxes and wire entanglements. The Allies had to take both spurs before they could capture Passchendaele. Bellevue Spur was to come later; at the moment New Zealand Division's objective was Gravenstafel. Although some tanks were to be used in the attack there were none in the II Anzac Corps sector. Environment and German artillery made the Ypres area a tank graveyard.

New Zealanders planned to attack in two stages. Stage One was to get to the Red Line. It ran roughly along the crest of the ridge just short of Gravenstafel village. Four battalions would attack German trenches, shell holes and pillboxes up to this Red Line. Stage Two was to get to the Blue Line. It was at the bottom of Bellevue Spur about 500 metres east of Gravenstafel and closer to Passchendaele. Four more battalions would leapfrog the first four battalions and get to the Blue Line.

POELCAPPELLE

PASSCHEN

BELLEVUE

ST JULIEN

HANEBEEK STREAM

GRAVENSTAFEL

NEW ZEALAND DIVISION

ABRAHAM HEIGHTS

HILL 40

ZONNEBEKE

BROODSEINDE

POLYGON WOOD

GHELUVELT

FRONT LINE OF MORNING OF OCTOBER 4

FRONT LINE OF EVENING OF OCTOBER 4

EXPLAIN/ DESCRIBE/ DISCUSS ... possible differences between leaders wh planned the attack and soldiers who waited in trenches.

NET: Find out what other divisions were to be involved in this attack.

BLOG: Update your blog.

October 4 Attack

Focus
- People move between places which has results for people and places.
- Events have causes and effects.

At 6 am on October 4, in a cold and windy drizzle, an artillery barrage of field guns and howitzers opened up. Its wall of flame and long, huge roar made the air quiver. It deafened the New Zealanders. They leapt from trenches and advanced towards the Germans.

In order to surprise the Germans, there had been no bombardment before the attack. The Germans had been quiet for their own reason. A German division was down in the dark marshes of the Hanebeek stream. The division was creeping silently into position for a dawn attack. The 6 o'clock barrage beat them by about ten minutes. Now the barrage cut the German division down. It also disrupted German organisation so all day the Germans struggled to keep up with what was happening.

Despite the change in weather, the ground stayed stable enough for artillery to give excellent support during the battle. It also meant infantry had reasonably solid ground and not mud underfoot.

The first 200 metres was easy for the New Zealanders. The opening barrage killed many Germans who were in the open with bayonets fixed. Stunned survivors fell to New Zealand bayonets. Many Germans surrendered. This let New Zealanders throw grenades into pillboxes. The Germans rallied and their machine guns jumped into deadly operation. However, the first four battalions reached the Red Line on schedule. They dug in and waited for the next battalions to leapfrog them. The artillery barrage continued.

Many New Zealanders were killed during the advance over Abraham Heights. By 11 am, on time, battalions reached the Blue Line. They dug in. Germans attacked them several times. Each time New Zealanders pushed them back.

EXPLAIN/ DESCRIBE/ DISCUSS ... why the New Zealanders fought this battle and what caused the event.

NET: Read at least three accounts of the battle of Broodseinde. An Australian soldier won a prize for essay writing with his account. Try to find it.

BLOG: Update your blog.

Results of Broodseinde

Focus
• Events have causes and effects.

British military planners believed the battle was a great victory. The policy of 'bite and hold' had defeated the Germans. All German counter-attacks to win back lost ground failed.

It rained on October 5. Soldiers in the forward trenches were knee-deep in mud and water. Yet Broodseinde showed what the New Zealand Division could do. It had the record of being the only Allied division which had always taken its objectives, always done it on time and never lost the places it had taken.

Some unwounded German prisoners were used to carry injured sol...

Newspapers in New Zealand said Anzacs fought like tigers and helped hand out Germany's biggest defeat.

New Zealanders had advanced the line by about 2,000 metres. Gravenstafel Spur was a top gain. From there New Zealanders could see pillboxes on Bellevue Spur. Although still beyond range of most Allied guns, Passchendaele village was now less than three kms away.

It took stretcher-bearers three days to clear the battlefield. New Zealanders had killed many Germans and captured about 1,160. They could see German stretcher-bearers up on Bellevue Spur collecting their wounded. New Zealanders suffered 1,853 casualties. About 450 of these were deaths. Among the dead was former All Black captain Dave Gallaher. He had signed up for service after his younger brother had been killed in action. After training at Sling Camp, he went to the Western Front. As Sergeant, he took his men over the top at Broodseinde. A German shot him in the face. He was carried to a clearing station in a tunnel. Later in the day he died.

On October 6 a British division relieved the New Zealanders who went back into the Salient to wait for further orders. They were exhausted but still had a long march to an area west of Ypres. After three sleepless nights, the went to their billets.

EXPLAIN/ DESCRIBE/ DISCUSS ... reasons for the success of Broodseinde, and results of the attack.

NET: Find out how many other ex-All Blacks were killed on the Western Front during World War I.

BLOG: Update your blog.

Eyes on Passchendaele

Focus

- Events have causes and effects.

An important result of Broodseinde was that military planners kept their eyes fixed on taking Passchendaele ridge and ruined village. They wanted to keep attacking Germans in Flanders until Passchendaele was captured. They thought October 4 had shocked Germans and that a final push would clear them out of the Passchendaele area. German morale was low. A German regiment that New Zealanders attacked recorded that October 4 was the blackest day in the history of the regiment and German losses were very heavy. The state of German prisoners suggested the Germans were in trouble. Some were only 16 and many were shorter than five feet (1.5m) tall.

For another push to Passchendaele, the major need was roading. New Zealand Engineers and Pioneers did not go back to the rear. They were left in the battle area. They had to keep building tracks and roads.

At night carters brought in timber. In day-time builders constructed roading. Both carters and builders spent a lot of time fixing up holes that German shells kept making. They also spent a lot of time digging out British lorries from mud in which drivers had stuck them.

Even in the rear, conditions were terrible. Men trudged off in wind and rain to do a day's work in mud. They returned in more rain to their bivouacs on ground that was nearly a lake. Down they lay in clothes and blankets that had not been dry for days. Above them came German bombing planes. Every night bombers killed some soldiers in crowded camps.

On October 9 another push to capture Passchendaele took place. It became known as the Battle of Poelcappelle. The New Zealand infantry were not involved. The battle was a failure for the Allies. Haig ordered another attack to take Passchendaele on October 12. This time II Anzac Corps was to make the main effort. New Zealand Division was to go into battle again.

EXPLAIN/ DESCRIBE/ DISCUSS ... how the results of Broodseinde were linked to the cause of the October 12 battle.

NET: Find out about the battle of Poelcappelle.

BLOG: Update your blog.

New Zealanders Get Ready

Focus
- Events have causes and results.
- People move between places which has results for people and places.

New Zealanders got orders to go to the front line. At dusk they left their billets at Pilckem. They had many kilometres to march. Rain pelted down. Anyone slipping off duckboards could drown in mud. It took about four hours to go about one and half kilometres. Once they were off duckboards it took four hours to go a quarter of that distance. Soldiers who lost the track were waist-high in mud and needed three or four others to drag them out.

On October 10 New Zealand infantry began to relieve troops of the British 49th Division. The New Zealand assembly area was roughly where the October 4 Blue Line had been. The 49th Division had failed in the October 9 battle to advance the front line. Now they were disorganised. British and German corpses, and dead horses and mules, still lay in the muck. The 49th had not dug trenches. They had just put two or three soldiers into each shell hole in a line. The area was now a swamp and close to German guns firing shells. German wire entanglements and pillboxes were still almost all undamaged.

New Zealand patrols immediately went out. Down at the swollen Ravebeek men were building bridges across the stream. They covered them with coconut matting to give a decent footing. The New Zealanders could see how bad things looked for soldiers who would have to cross those bridges and attack Germans who still had strong protection. Everything now depended on artillery support for the New Zealanders. Especially important would be the ability of artillery to cut wire entanglements.

The New Zealanders had to dig in and wait. In the cold they got little sleep. Breakfast of bread and bully beef was welcome. It rained off and on all day.

New Zealand troops on the way to the firing line.

New Zealand Engineers resting in a large shell hole.

New Zealand Division Headquarters were behind, on Yser Canal. It got command of the sector on October 11. 3rd Brigade was on the left of the sector and 2nd Brigade on the right. 4th Brigade was the reserve. 1st Brigade had replaced 3rd Brigade on engineering jobs.

The men of 3rd Brigade were exhausted. For over a month they had engineered, mostly at night, sometimes in gas masks under shell-fire. They had suffered 200 casualties. They also had not had pre-battle training as other brigades had. Stretcher-bearers were also tired out. Clearing stations were filling already because bearers were having to collect wounded soldiers who had been left by the 49th Division.

EXPLAIN/ DESCRIBE/ DISCUSS ... the situation that New Zealand Division inherited from the 49th Division.

NET: Other divisions in this battle were two Australian divisions and five British divisions. Check out where their starting lines were.

BLOG: Update your blog.

The Gun Problem

- Events have causes and results.
- People move between places which has results for people and places.

New Zealand Engineers and Pioneer Maori Battalion had tried to rep[a]
roads and tracks to the front line. A tram line to Gravenstafel to send
up ammunition and bring back the wounded would have been helpf[ul]
Lack of time and bad weather made it impossible to build.

Mules carrying ammunition to New Zealand guns.

Gun crew struggling in mud.

Winning ground from Germans on October 4 meant New Zealand Artillery with mules and horses had to shift guns forward. Otherwise guns would fire on their own infantry. Huge numbers of men dragged gun teams forward. Horses struggled, mud up to their bellies. Exhausted men slid down and slept in the rain.

It took hours and hours to move shells up to gun lines. When an animal got stuck in mud men had to take off its load of eight shells, haul the animal out, and load it again. One mule sank in a shell hole and men, using long rods to prod the hole, could not find it.

On October 4 sixty big guns went into action in the opening barrage. By October 12 only thirty eight were available. It took time and a hard surface to make proper gun platforms for big guns to sit on. With so much time and energy spent on shifting guns forward, there was not much time to make sure platforms were stable. After firing a few rounds, guns would become useless because recoil pushed them deeper into the mud.

Each artillery battery should have had thousands of rounds of ammunition. By October 12 most had a few hundred only. Mud also meant that every round had to be cleaned before firing. There was little clean water for this.

Bad weather grounded planes. This meant troops on the ground had no way of knowing where shells landed and where enemy positions were.

EXPLAIN/ DESCRIBE/ DISCUSS ... how successful the attack was likely to be.

NET: One method of repairing roads was 'fascines'. Find out what they are and how men at Passchendaele used them.

BLOG: Update your blog.

First Passchendaele, October 12

Focus

- Events have causes and results.
- People move between places which has results for people and places.

New Zealanders were ordered to attack at 5.30 am on October 12. Their main objective was Goudberg Spur. Soldiers were arranged in lines. This was hard to do in the dark, cold and rain. They were told to lie down and wait. They knew Australian and British soldiers in their sectors were also waiting. At 5.25 am they attacked. They could not even see Goudberg Spur. They knew ahead of them were Germans protected by pillboxes, by hidden machine gun posts and by belts of wire entanglements. What they did not know, and what experts now believe, is that Germans knew of the coming attack and had strengthened their line with more regiments and machine-guns. In this battle, on one side were exhausted soldiers struggling through mud and water in pouring rain. On the other side were soldiers waiting in concrete shelters, armed with machine-guns and protected with wire entanglements in front of them.

The opening barrage was so weak New Zealanders hardly noticed it. Shells dropped short. New Zealanders, under fire from their own shells, suffered casualties. Survivors had to wait for the barrage to lift. German artillery and machine-guns pounded Ravebeek Valley. Advancing New Zealanders fell. German snipers hiding in shell holes and behind tree stumps took out other New Zealanders. Artillery failed to cut German barbed wire. It also failed to knock out German pillboxes. As New Zealanders struggled waist deep in mud, German machine-gun fire picked them off. Many soldiers who fell in the swamp drowned. Some, with terrible injuries, crawled to the top of a crater where Germans shot them again.

By full daylight, survivors knew they had lost the battle. Too many men were dead. For example, a company of 1st Otago had 28 men left out of 140 who began the attack. Survivors slid into shell holes and waited. Germans shot anyone who showed his head. Rain poured down. Bullets whined. German shells sprayed shrapnel. Communication between the front line and leaders broke down. In the afternoon orders came for another push. This was postponed and then cancelled. Soldiers fell back to their start line. Wounded lay out in the mud. Many died before stretcher-bearers found them.

The New Zealanders had showed amazing courage. No infantry in the world could have reached Goudberg Spur that day. Yet they had advanced, many to their death. They were heroes.

PASSCHENDAELE 12 OCTOBER 1917

NZ POSITIONS
FRONT LINE
MAIN ROAD

POELCAPPELLE
GOUDBERG
PILCKEM
RAVEBEEK STREAM
STROMBEEK STREAM
BELLEVUE
PASSCH
GRAVENSTAFEL
BERLIN WOOD
ABRAHAM HEIGHTS
BROODS
POLYGON WOOD
MENIN ROAD

STROMBEEK STREAM
3RD NZ RIFLE BRIGADE
FRONT LINE
RAVEBE
NEW ZEALAND POSITIONS AT THE START OF THE BATTLE
2ND NZ INFANTRY BRIGADE
BE
WO

EXPLAIN/ DESCRIBE/ DISCUSS ... the actions of New Zealand soldiers on October 12

NET: Find some first-hand accounts of this battle.

BLOG: Update your blog.

Why Passchendaele is Important

Focus

- People pass on and look after culture and heritage.

This is what a New Zealand war correspondent wrote about the battle. It was published by *The New Zealand Herald*.

'The weather has been simply appalling. The battlefield has been such a sea of mud and of waterlogged shell holes that the continued success of our last attack was an utter impossibility.

At dawn thousands of fine-spirited New Zealanders flung themselves against heavily fortified enemy positions on Bellevue Spur, an ugly V-shaped hill extending a thousand yards back into Passchendaele township.

The enemy barrage played heavily upon them for twenty minutes before the start, but the lads rose eagerly from their line of shell holes and began a steady advance in wave formation, our barrage plunging ahead.

The men sank sometimes to the waist in the deep mud. The barrage went faster than the advance possibly could. The enemy machine-gun fire swelled to a shriek. Many fell, but the men pressed on.

They reached the Rabapeek (Ravebeek) Creek and plunged into this deep morass. The enemy's main barrage of shrapnel and high explosive descended hereabouts, while the trenches between the concrete redoubts, seemed to close the passage over the stone road which traverses the morass.

The men, nevertheless, pressed irresistibly over the dead across the road, others plunging through the water, though wounded. Some were drowned.

The ascent of the slope began. The first wave, now thin, reached the wire. The gallant lads tried every means of piercing it. Wave after wave advanced to death. Many were riddled with bullets. Others dropped to the ground and began crawling beneath the wire. Many who were shot remained, but some reached the other side, charged and fell.

The waves had determindedly expended themselves. The survivors remained in the shell holes, awaiting another effort, which the commanders decided was not desirable to make.

The stretcher bearers never worked more heroically than they did today, their difficulties being increased owing to mud and the long distances over which the wounded had to be carried.

The Germans, finding their Red Cross respected, gave the New Zealand stretcher bearers a safe passage. At one time 300 stretcher cases were lying outside a New Zealand aid post in full view of the enemy. Not a shot was fired.'

EXPLAIN/ DESCRIBE/ DISCUSS … how Passchendaelle, like Gallipoli, helped New Zealanders have a sense of national identity.

NET: By the time New Zealand Division was finally withdrawn from the Ypres front line in 1918, it had over 18,000 casualties, including about 5,000 deaths. It won three Victoria Crosses. Find out about each VC.

BLOG: Update your blog.

The Human Cost

Focus
- Events have causes and results.
- People move between places which has results for people and places.

THE CASUALTY LIST.

In just two hours, 2,846 New Zealand soldiers were killed, wounded or listed as missing. Most of those listed as missing had been killed but their bodies were never found. Another 138 died of their wounds over the next week. Experts say that if you add sickness to the casualties, the New Zealand Division lost almost 7,500 men during October 1917.

In 1917 the population of New Zealand was just over a million. Passchendaele affected the whole society since so many people knew someone or of someone in casualty lists. Some lost more than one. Charles, Edwin and Leslie Newlove from Takaka did not come home. Charles went missing in the October 4 attack. Edwin and Leslie fell in the October 12 attack.

Evacuating casualties from the battlefield was a nightmare for stretcher-bearers. On October 13 every man in the division helped carry in wounded. It took six to eight bearers to get each stretcher to a dressing station. Four hours to go less than five kilometres made feet so swollen and sore many bearers had to cut off their boots. Mud caked uniforms up to armpits. Eyes were bloodshot. It was not until the afternoon of October 14 that all wounded were taken from the battlefield.

The wounded had a terrible time also. Many died before stretcher-bearers found them. Many died when shells exploded on dressing stations. If stations were full, wounded lay outside, sinking into mud in the rain. Injuries, such as stumps left where arms or legs had been, caused horrific pain. Aspirin was not strong enough but the on other pain-killer was a morphine injection. As it caused unconsciousness it was given only in extreme cases.

Survivors had physical and mental scars. They had learned too many terrible things. Many could never talk abou what happened. Some were haunted by images such as the face of their best mate being shot off. Many had constant nightmares. Some had nervous breakdowns.

EXPLAIN/ DESCRIBE/ DISCUSS ... how an event such as Passchendaele has a human cost

NET: Find the number of New Zealanders killed on October 12 at Passchendaele, on six different internet sites, and comment on any differences you find.

BLOG: Update your blog.

Other Results of October 12

Focus
- Events have causes and results.
- People move between places which has results for people and places.

The attack was a disaster in all sectors. No objectives were taken. At most it had carried the British front line forward in some places between 200 to 500 metres. For the first time in this campaign New Zealand soldiers had failed. It damaged their morale. When they got word to leave the Passchendaele swamp they were relieved.

Attackers – British, New Zealanders, Australians – lost their confidence. German morale, however, rose.

The days of 1914 when soldiers and civilians saw war as a glorious adventure, had long gone. It seemed war would last forever. New Zealand troops were exhausted and many were sick. They had been expected to be superhuman. The main New Zealand Hospital in Britain, Brockenhurst in Hampshire, had so many admissions it ran out of bed space.

Passchendaele showed once again the gap between soldiers and their top leaders. Leaders did not climb out of trenches with soldiers. They did not go out and look at the place to which they were sending soldiers. Soldiers had to obey orders to attack without question. New Zealand soldiers saw differences between the British class system and New Zealand's developing society where social class was not so evident.

Passchendaele was New Zealand's greatest human catastrophe. It affected more Kiwi families on a single day than any other event in history. Families of dead soldiers had no body to bury, and no grave with a headstone to visit.

New Zealand heroes of Passchendaele would have featured in Field-Marshal Haig's later comment: 'The Empire is proud of the part which New Zealand is playing in this war and no troops could have fought more gallantly than the New Zealand Division.' Many survivors were upset at the loss of so many comrades whom, they said, had died for nothing.

EXPLAIN/ DESCRIBE/ DISCUSS ... how Passchendaele had many results.

NET: Find out when, how and why the Western Front closed down.

BLOG: Update your blog.

Passchendaele is Part of our Culture and Heritage

Focus
- People pass on and look after culture and heritage.
- Cultural interaction impacts on cultures and societies.

After a major event like Passchendaele people want to honour those involved, along with their actions, and make sure they are not forgotten. Kiwis involved in Passchendaele have become part of New Zealand's culture and heritage. One result is that more and more New Zealanders are learning about Passchendaele.

Many Kiwis go to see Passchendaele memorials in Belgium. They take photographs to show people back home. They talk to locals. In this way people of Belgium and New Zealand see each other's cultures and strengthen bonds between their countries.

People from New Zealand who were involved in Passchendaele saw other cultures, such as the British and Australian, Belgian and French. They sent letters and postcards home. Those who survived and those who died had an impact on their families and societies.

Passchendaele was part of the broader Western Front experience for New Zealand soldiers. For many, the war brought them overseas for the first time. Getting to know other cultures helped them think of themselves as Kiwis because they noticed differences between other cultures and their own. At the end of the war some soldiers cut a huge drawing of a kiwi into the hillside above Sling Camp. You can still see it today.

New Zealanders today are proud of Kiwi soldiers at Passchendaele. Kiwis did not stage a mutiny because conditions were tough. They dug deep in both senses and got on with it.

EXPLAIN/ DESCRIBE/ DISCUSS ... what cultural interaction is and how Passchendaele is part of New Zealand's cultural interaction.

NET: Find a picture of the Sling kiwi.

BLOG: Update your blog.

How Passchendaele is Remembered in Belgium

Focus
- People pass on and look after culture and heritage.
- Cultural interaction impacts on cultures and societies.

Tyne Cot cemetry in Belgium.

Among trees beside the road at Gravenstafel is a stone monument. It overlooks the slope up which New Zealanders attacked on October 4 1917. Engraved on the monument is a badge with a fern leaf and 'New Zealand' over crossed taiaha. The image has a frame of Maori carving. The base says, 'From the Uttermost Ends of the Earth.' You can walk from here to Passchendaele in half an hour. In 1917 troops took several weeks.

A cemetery called Tyne Cot is located between Broodseinde and Passchendaele. It began in October 1917 when Allies used a captured German pillbox as an advanced dressing station and buried soldiers there. Today almost 12,000 soldiers lie there. About 70 percent are unknown. There are 520 New Zealand headstones. 322 New Zealand headstones have the words 'Known Unto God' because their names are unknown. There are probably many more New Zealanders among those buried whose nationality could not be worked out. There is also a New Zealand Memorial to the Missing. It has the names of 1,179 New Zealanders killed at Passchendaele who have no known grave. It says, 'Here are recorded the names of the officers and men of New Zealand who fell in the Battle of Broodseinde and the first Battle of Passchendaele, October 1917, and whose graves are known only to God.'

There are another two New Zealand Memorials to the Missing. They are at Polygon Wood and Messines. New Zealanders are also buried in places such as the British Nine Elms cemetery. This is because many men lay in mud for hours before stretcher-bearers found them. Many died from wounds before they reached hospitals and so were buried at the nearest place. At Menin Gate stands a Hall of Memory with names of soldiers engraved on it. It includes New Zealanders who were killed serving with British or Australian forces. Each night at 8 pm traffic is stopped while members of the local Fire Brigade on the road under the Memorial's arches sound the Last Post. Visitors today can go on a tour to the Ypres Salient and see German trenches, 'Shot at Dawn' execution sites, places of the first German gas attack and flame throwers attack, and a dugout. On the Western Front farms today the harvest of iron continues as farmers dig up weaponry from the war. The harvest of bones also continues as farmers dig up pieces of skeletons.

EXPLAIN/ DESCRIBE/ DISCUSS ... places you could visit in Belgium to find out more about New Zealanders at Passchendaele.

NET: Find pictures of the cemeteries and memorials mentioned above.

BLOG: Update your blog.

How Passchendaele is Remembered in New Zealand

Focus

- Events have causes and results.
- People move between places which has results for people and places.

Historians at the New Zealand Ministry for Culture and Heritage have a website that features archival film, photos, stories and oral histories about Passchendaele.

Digitised Casualty Forms of New Zealanders killed at Passchendaele were recently presented to the Minister of Veterans' Affairs by Archives NZ. They are part of the Passchendaele Project, a commemoration dedicated to the Kiwi soldiers who lost their lives on October 12. The Forms give details of service, next of kin, and place of burial. Passchendaele appears in some street names. It is part of the RSA red poppy, Anzac Day services, RSA Halls and war memorials.

The Army Museum at Waiouru with its Kippenberger Military Archives and Research Library has material on Passchendaele including photographs. The Alexander Turnbull Library has many photographs of Passchendaele.

More students at school today are learning about Passchendaele. New Zealand appointed three official war artist towards the end of the war. Although their paintings were censored, like letters from soldiers, they painted some Passchendaele events. Their paintings are now part of New Zealand's culture and heritage.

There are memorials about Passchendaele in a few places such as Central Railway Station in Christchurch.

Passchendaele is the subject of books, poems and songs. There are, for example, many versions of the following Soldier's Song. A whizz-bang was a light shell fired from a small field artillery gun. It flew through the air with a whizzing noise.

> Far, far from Ypres I long to be
> Where German snipers can't snipe at me
> Damp is my dugout,
> Cold are my feet,
> Waiting for whizz-bangs
> To send me to sleep.

EXPLAIN/ DESCRIBE/ DISCUSS ... how Passchendaele is part of our culture and heritage

NET: Find the names and authors of some books about Passchendaele.

BLOG: Update your blog.